Dorothy Day

Dorothy's Journey

The Young Life of Dorothy Day

Claire Mohan and Patricia Gallagher

Patricia C. Gallagher
Young Sparrow Press
P.O. Box 561
Worcester, PA 19490
www.patriciausa.com
Phone: (267) 939 0365

The authors welcome interviews and speaking engagements. Books are available for bulk sales and can be customized to meet your needs.

Published by Young Sparrow Press
P.O. Box 561
Worcester, PA 19490

(267) 939-0365

Library of Congress-in-Publication Data
Mohan, Claire Jordan
Dorothy's Journey, The Young Life of Dorothy Day
Claire Jordan Mohan – 1st ed.

ISBN 13 978 1493749744

Printed in the United States of America

Cover art and illustrations by Sonja Fafaj

Contents

Prologue: ix

1.   The Beginning   1

2.   Off to California   5

3.   The Earthquake   9

4.   Chicago   13

5.   Busy Days   17

6.   Adolescence   21

7.   Changes of Direction   23

8.   Finding a Way   25

9.   God's Call   27

10. Nursing   29

11. Moving On   35

12. Lonely Days   41

13. A New Direction   43

14. Final Days   49

     Notes   53

     Sayings   54

     Chronology   56

     The Corporal Works of Mercy   58

     The Spiritual Works of Mercy   59

     The Sermon on the Mount   60

     Other Works by Claire Jordan Mohan   62

I fled Him down the nights and down the days
I fled Him down the arches of the years
I fled Him down the labyrinthine ways
Of my own mind; and in the midst of tears
I hid from Him.

The Hound of Heaven, Francis Thompson

Prologue

Suffer the little children to come unto me, and forbid them not; for of such is the Kingdom of Heaven.
— Matthew 10:14.

The girls had worked hard all day helping their mothers with the housework and taking care of their little brothers and sisters. They sat there savoring some fresh fruit and stretching their legs. "Oh, Mary, my back is aching," Dorothy cried.

"Mine, too," her friend replied.

It was a warm evening. A summer shower had pelted them with rain and chased away the heat, but the sky now was clear. The lightning and thunder had disappeared and all was still. A sliver of moon shone down on the two girls. Mary edged closer to the front steps to get a clearer view of the bright stars.

Twelve-year-old Mary gazed up at the sky and said, "I wonder what heaven is like?"

Eight-year-old Dorothy was too young to have ever pondered this question. She wrinkled her nose. "Mary, what's heaven? How do we get there?" she asked.

Mary moved to a lower creaking step. She stared at Dorothy and then at the twinkling stars. She closed her eyes for a moment, then she answered solemnly, "You have to be a saint!"

Dorothy pushed her hair from her eyes, looked at her friend, and questioned, "What's that? What is a saint?"

"Don't worry, Dor, I can tell you all about them," Mary answered. "They teach us about them at church."

Dorothy cocked her head and moved to the step to be close to her friend. She bit into a juicy peach. Her eyes never left Mary's face as she listened to stories of the wonderful deeds that were done by brave and holy men and women. Mary said it was all because they loved God and spent all their lives serving Him. At that moment, something stirred inside Dorothy.

"They are people who loved God and who helped the poor. They talked about God to the crowds and even gave up their lives for Him," said Mary

Her heart almost burst with desire to be like them. "Oh, Mary," she cried "I want to be a saint!"

She didn't know why, but she found herself whispering to a God she hardly knew, "Thank you, God. Oh, thank you for Mary."

Later that week, Dorothy went to her friend Kathryn's apartment next-door to ask her out to play. She climbed up the wooden porch steps and knocked at the door. No one answered, so she slid it open and wandered into the tiny kitchen. Though a cup of tea sat on the table, no one was there. Dorothy made her way through the rooms searching everywhere, calling, "Kathy, Kathy!" No one answered. When she came to the front bedroom, she saw Mrs. Barrett down on her knees by the side of her bed with her hands folded, praying. As Dorothy bounded into the room, the woman jumped and turned her head.

"Oh, Dorothy," she said. "Kathryn will be right back. She just went to the store. Now you must go to the parlor and wait for her."

Then Mrs. Barrett seemed to forget the little girl and returned to her prayers. Once again, Dorothy was puzzled. She had never seen anyone deeply in prayer before. "Oh, my," she thought, "This must be what saints do." She *now* knew how to be a saint!

Dorothy knew little about God. Her family did not go to church or talk about Him, but for some reason every night before she said good-night, her mother would have her clasp her hands and pray, "Now I lay me down to sleep . . ." and "Bless my father and my mother . . ." She didn't pay much attention to what she was saying as she kissed her mama, closed her eyes and drifted off to sleep.

Although Dorothy knew right from wrong, she didn't have any thoughts of God unless there was a thunderstorm. Then, as the lightning streaked across the sky and the thunder boomed, she hid her head under the soft covers and whispered for His help.

This story will tell you about the long, long way this little girl traveled and the years that passed before she actually found out who this God was, as well as how she learned to follow Him in her life.

Chapter 1

The Beginning

Gladness of the heart is the life of a man, and the
joyfulness of man prolongeth his days.
— Psalm 4:7.

Dorothy Day was born November 8, 1897 in Brooklyn Heights, New York. Her mother, Grace Satterlee, a dark-haired beauty, was studying at a business school in the city when she met John Day, a handsome sportswriter for a New York City newspaper. He could not resist her sweetness and beauty and she was captivated by his charm. They fell in love and soon were married at the Perry Street Episcopal Church in Greenwich Village.

They had a happy life together and were blessed by God. Within a year Dorothy's brother Donald was born, followed by Sam, Dorothy, her sister Della, and another brother, John. Their father wrote for a morning newspaper so he worked throughout the night and slept in the daytime.

The children seldom saw him, but they were very close to their mother and her family. At night, while at the table eating their evening meal, Mama used to tell them about "when she was a little girl." Dorothy never stirred, for she loved to hear every detail about Aunt Cassie and her grandparents and the fun the family had skating and ice-boating on the Hudson River during the cold winters when her mother was young.

This loving family lived in the borough of Brooklyn until Dorothy was six years old. Although Dorothy's mother had been an Episcopalian, her father did not believe in God. Other than the bedtime prayer there was no religious instruction in their house and they never went to church. Dorothy did pray when she started public school. Each morning before class started, the children sat at their little desks with their hands folded. When the bell rang, the teacher would lead them as they bowed their heads and said the Lord's Prayer. So she learned a little about prayer . . . but still nothing about God.

The children did have good times together. Donald, Sam and Dorothy loved to go to the nearby river where they went fishing for eels. Often, along with their cousin, they ran off to play in an abandoned shack in a swamp around a nearby fort.

"Let's pretend we are going to live here by ourselves forever," suggested Don one day as they tramped toward home carrying their buckets.

"Oh, yes!" Sam and Dorothy shouted as they ran beside him.

The next day, they cleaned out the shack, ran around the swamp, and pulled some weeds. It became "their home" and they played there every chance they could get.

Dorothy loved adventure and one day decided to go to the shack by herself. It was a sunny afternoon, but after a few hours the sky darkened. Suddenly, she realized she was alone and it was almost night. A grim fear overwhelmed her. She grabbed her things and ran all the way home. Her mother was standing in the doorway with her arms outstretched.

"Dorothy, where have you been? I've been looking all over for you," she said as she held Dorothy close.

Dorothy had tears in her eyes as she snuggled against her mother, the wetness soaking her mother's shirt. The next time she went to the shack, it was with her brothers by her side.

Chapter 2

Off to California

Many waters cannot quench love, neither can the floods drown it.
— *Song of Solomon 8:7*

When Dorothy was seven-years-old her father got a new job as a sportswriter for a newspaper in California, writing a column on horse racing. So they packed up and moved, first, for a short time, to Berkeley as they awaited their furniture which was being shipped, and then on to Oakland where her father had found a beautiful home surrounded by trees and flowers. Life was happy there with many hours playing with her brothers, exploring the area and sharing the fun boys like to have. But at times this little girl would go off by herself and do girl things. She read little story books, worked in the garden, pulled weeds and plucked the flowers. She would make dolls out of calla lilies with roses for heads, making up stories to herself as she played with them.

As with most girls who like to try new things, she would crush flowers and put them in bottles of water to make perfume and give them to her mother.

"Look, Mama, now you will smell pretty," Dorothy would say. Her mother would splash some on her arms.

"Oh, thank you, sweetie. This smells so good. Where did you get it?" she would ask.

"Oh, Mama, I made it just for you," said Dorothy with a laugh and her mother would smile.

On fun days with the boys, Dorothy, a little tomboy, enjoyed playing with dirt and sand, watching anthills and finding gopher holes, just like her brothers. Sometimes she would wander to a brook, take off her shoes and sit on a rock, dipping her toes in the cool water. She would listen quietly to the music of the stream as it caressed her feet. Or she might catch some tadpoles swimming nearby, put them in a little pail, and take them home to her brothers.

"Don, Sam!" she would call out as she ran down the path to their house. "Look what I have!"

The boys would grab the pail and quickly put the little creatures in a bowl. Every day they would check them, watching as they gradually lost their tails, got legs, and become frogs.

When he saw this happening, Don would grab her hand and say, "Come on, Dorothy, it's time to take them back to the creek. Any minute they will start jumping out of the bowl and hopping around the house and you know Mama wouldn't like that."

They would quickly put them in a bucket and head for the water. Dorothy smiled as they trudged along, her brothers complaining as she stopped to pick daisies along the way.

"Mama will love these pretty flowers," she told the boys, but they were interested in other things.

Somehow she felt that the beauty around her came from God, but she didn't really understand who He was.

As she grew older, there were other things that made her wonder about God. In Berkeley they lived in an old house with an attic packed with mysterious things. Now that she could read a little she would climb up there on Sunday afternoons and look through the Bible she had found hidden under an eave. Only eight-years-old, she didn't understand much that she read, but she just felt holy with the book in her hands. She knew it was special.

At that time they lived next to a Methodist family who had a little store with an apartment in the back.

On Sunday mornings, Birdie, her neighbor, would call to her, "Dorothy, would you like to go to Sunday school and church with me?"

Mama did not object, so Dorothy would say, "I'll be right there, Birdie," as she ran to put on her prettiest flowered dress and shiny patent leather shoes. She learned the hymns and prayed with the congregation as they lifted their hearts to God.

One afternoon when she returned from services, she sat on a stool in the kitchen as her mother was preparing dinner.

"Mama, why don't we pray and go to church and sing hymns?" she asked. Her mother just turned her head away, tossed the salad, and continued to stir their dinner on the stove. Without an answer, her mother changed the subject . . . and so Dorothy continued to have questions that wouldn't be answered for many years.

Chapter 3

The Earthquake

Love is the measure by which we will be judged.
— *Dorothy Day.*

The city of San Francisco was asleep on April 18, 1906, at 5:12 A.M., when a very powerful earthquake shook the area. Violent shocks punctuated by strong shaking lasted only about 45 to 60 seconds. The city went up in flames. Over 700 people died, with 250,000 homeless. Four hundred city blocks and 25,000 buildings were destroyed. The earthquake began with a deep rumbling. The convulsions continued afterward, so that the ground became like a sea that rocked the entire area, including the Day home which was across the San Francisco Bay in Oakland. Even at that distance there was a large windmill and water tank in back of the house that sent the water splashing from the tank onto the top of their roof.

As soon as the rumble started, Mr. Day took the boys from their beds and rushed to the front door, where his wife waited with Della, whom she snatched from Dorothy's bed. Strangely, in the confusion, nobody rescued Dorothy. She was left in a big brass bed, which rolled back and forth and back and forth on the polished hardwood floor. She didn't know what was happening so she climbed out of bed and ran to the hallway. She was shivering and shaking as she ran, slipping and sliding down the stairs until she was finally able to reach her parents.

"How could we have forgotten you?" Papa and Mama said as they wiped her tears and hugged her. "We love you, Dorothy. We are so sorry you were so frightened."

She clung to them sobbing and wondering what had happened to the world. She felt death around her. When she finally fell asleep her ears seemed to burst with a great thunder that became louder and louder and approached nearer and nearer until she woke up again screaming and sweating with fear.

"Mama, Mama, help me!" she called out. Her mother who sat beside her, wrapped her arms around her little girl and comforted her. "There, there, dear. Don't be afraid. Mama's here."

When the earth settled, the city of San Francisco was destroyed. Its buildings, shaken and tossed, had moved and collapsed. Everything was in chaos. Fires were blazing everywhere and the streets were sunken down three or four feet into the ground or had humps towering four or five feet high.

The Day's house across the bay in Oakland was ruined, dishes broken all over the floor, books out of their bookcases, chandeliers down, chimneys fallen, and the house was cracked from roof to ground. The city of San Francisco was burning, but there were no fires in Oakland. Yet the flames and banks of smoke could be seen across the bay.

People were confused and lost. All the next day they crossed the water by ferry and by boat. A camping ground was set up for the new arrivals. Mrs. Day and her neighbor gave them clothes and food and found them places to stay. Dorothy was with her mother all day, doing everything that a little girl could, such as sharing her own things with the frightened children. The women gave their love and everything they had to comfort the refugees. All the while the earth continued to tremble. Everyone was fearful of what would happen next. Dorothy was frightened, too, and was afraid of God who was being blamed by the people around her.

Chapter 4

Chicago

You are my God . . . for You have been a refuge to the
poor, a refuge to the needy in their distress.
— *Isaiah 25:1-4*

The newspaper plant where Mr. Day worked was destroyed when it went up in flames. Since their father no longer had a job, the Days gathered the few belongings they had, took a train and left as quickly as they could. Within a week, they were on their way to Chicago to a start a strange new life in another city.

Her mother searched for an apartment, but since her father didn't have a job, money was scarce. The only place they could afford was dark and dingy. It had a few windows, one in the dining room facing Lake Michigan two blocks away, which looked out upon shabby shacks and railroad tracks. It was very different from their bungalow in Oakland, which had been a lovely place with lush trees, beautiful flowers, and rolling hills. Outside there was a yard of paved cement. There was nothing green to be seen except a sad-looking tree on a dirty vacant lot down at the corner.

A long, shaky porch ran along the front of the building where the many neighborhood children would jump rope, and play stone steps, hop scotch and other games at the end of the day. When it was quiet and the others had gone to bed, Mary Harrington, who became Dorothy's best friend, often sat with Dorothy on the front porch and told her about God, heaven, and the saints, but since Dorothy's father soon secured a good job as a sports editor, their days of poverty were over. The Days moved to a better neighborhood, and Dorothy lost contact with her friend.

However, before that happened, days were a difficult time for all the family. Dorothy's mother no longer had a housekeeper so she had to do all her own work, even washing clothes in a large common basement with all the other mothers. Through it all she never complained. Dorothy did all she could every day to help her mother, making curtain rods from fishing poles and finding orange crates for kitchen stools.

When they had been in Chicago for a month, Dorothy's father said to her mother, "Grace, I think it is time for me to take off and do some writing. You know I have been wanting to do this for a long time."

"John, you must do it," Grace agreed. "We'll be fine, don't worry."

So every day her father would sit in his comfortable chair with a table leaf over the arms to hold his typewriter as he smoked cigarette after cigarette and typed short stories which he sold to various magazines to feed his family and pay the rent.

Grace, who was proud of her husband, didn't worry when things were going badly, even though they were living in poverty. Somehow they managed to pay their bills and be happy with what they had.

Della and Dorothy didn't get out very much as their father did not want them to socialize with these poor uneducated people. They read a lot and spent time peering out the windows. The girls sat together for hours watching a man making and selling popcorn at a bright-colored stand under an umbrella on the corner. They watched him pop the corn, fill the bags, and add melted butter. They could smell it and almost taste it but there wasn't any for them. Their family's budget meant this was as close as they could get.

Chapter 5

Busy Days

Love for one's neighbor is the true path up to the Lord
because love is the stairway that leads to God.
— *Pope Benedict XVI*

One day, when Dorothy was ten-years-old, the rector from the nearby Episcopal Church stopped at the apartment while her father was sitting in the living room busily typing. The priest was visiting door-to-door to encourage the residents to join his church. He knocked on the door and spoke to Mr. Day.

"Good morning, sir," he said as he introduced himself to Dorothy's father, who had pushed his typewriter away and opened the door a crack. "I see you have some young sons. We would be happy to have your boys singing in our choir on Sunday and they could also play in the gymnasium during the week."

Mr. Day agreed, not because he had any religion, but because he did like the idea of his sons going to the gym.

"Dorothy, you may go with the boys to church," her father told her. So every Sunday, she happily went with her brothers. *Oh, how beautiful they look in their cassocks and surplices,* she thought. *I wish that I could be in the choir, too.*

During the service, Dorothy learned to love the Psalms and thought they were beautiful. She even went to Sunday school and studied the catechism expecting to be baptized and confirmed, but that was the end of her religious education because their poverty did not last very long.

Her father took a job as sports editor at *The Inter Ocean* newspaper and they moved to a larger apartment and finally to a beautiful house on the North Side of the city. Once again they had a home with fireplaces, comfortable furniture, and even a little desk for Dorothy in the corner of the living room. They would make hot cocoa over the fire before they went to bed at night and Mother would serve them warm, tasty bread that she had baked in her shiny new oven. Everything was calm and peaceful.

Chapter 6

Adolescence

Lead the life . . . to which God called you.
— *1 Corinthians 7:17*

In May of the year Dorothy was fourteen, a new baby was born. They called him John. Dorothy loved his big blue eyes, his little pink cheeks, and his tiny clenched fists. She loved his gurgling sounds and everything about him and was always ready to care for him. Since their mother was tired and a little depressed after his birth, Dorothy became his "little mother."

Her father did not get to bed until two in the morning, so her mother felt that it was very important that he get a good sleep. When the baby got a little older at about 4 o'clock every morning she would gently scoop the baby from his crib and tiptoe down the hall carrying him to his sister's bedroom. Dorothy would awaken and take him in her arms. *Oh, little John, I love you*, she told him. He always widened his eyes and smiled the minute he glimpsed his big sister. She rocked him and sang songs to settle him, but he was wide awake and just wanted to play. At dawn he would jump up and down, peep at the birds

21

outside his window, and chuckle and crow. Finally, she would change his diaper and run downstairs to get him a bottle. After draining the little bottle of warm milk he would roll over and go back to sleep. *Now that I am wide awake, I will do some homework,* Dorothy would think.

Although Dorothy would be tired herself, the hours she spent with that little baby just made her love him more. She was always with him. He was "her baby." Every day after school, in all seasons, she couldn't wait to get home to care for him. On cool winter days she would slip a little sweater or jacket on John, wrap him in a warm blanket, and place him in his stroller. Then they would take a walk to the park where it was all quiet and peaceful. He smiled at everyone he saw.

"What a cute little baby," older ladies would say as they tickled his chin. Dorothy smiled, too. She felt somehow God was in her little brother.

As she got older and was alone or her little brother was sleeping, Dorothy loved to read. There were no comic books, detective stories or what her parents called "trash books" around the house. They only were allowed to read books by classical authors. She also liked *Science and Health,* her mother's magazine, with its daily readings from the Bible. Still, she managed to get hold of some romance stories lent to her by friends at school, but she never dared to allow her father to see them.

Chapter 7

Changes of Direction

*The needy shall not always be forgotten, nor the hope of
the poor perish forever.*
— Psalm 9:18.

Her older brother Donald, like his father, began to
pursue a newspaper career, writing for a paper called
The Day Book. As Dorothy read the newspaper and his
articles, she learned of the struggles of the poor in Chicago.
She also read Carl Sandburg's poems and Jack London's
stories. After she read *The Jungle* by Upton Sinclair, a story
about life on the West Side of Chicago, she felt moved to
walk there. She pushed John's carriage for miles, dragging
her little sister along with her, as Della always wanted to be
at her side. They would go up and down the gray dirty
streets taking in all the poverty and sadness. As the years
passed she felt that somehow her life was linked with the
poor who lived there.

*I think God wants man to be happy and that he will
provide him with what he needs. I don't think we need to
have all this misery in the world,* she thought.

On the other hand, her parents had taught her that

the destitute were shiftless, worthless, without talent of any kind and that they were that way because of their own fault. Seeing all these people first hand set her to wonder. Could they help themselves? Why were the people she met at school and home not concerned about the poverty around them? Didn't they see these lost people? Although she had read Jesus' words in the Bible, she did not see anyone taking off his coat and giving it to the poor. She didn't see anyone having a banquet and calling in the lame, the halt, and the blind. What did this all mean? She wanted everyone to be kind as she remembered they had been in San Francisco after the earthquake.

Chapter 8

Finding a Way

I always had a sense of being followed, of being desired, a sense of hope and expectation.
— *Dorothy Day.*

A year later, when she was sixteen, Dorothy won a scholarship to the university. She was happy and excited at leaving home and being independent. She made new friends and studied hard, but after a few months, she suffered from a terrible homesickness. She missed her two-year-old brother whom she loved beyond anyone or anything. *Dorothy, you must get over this. Things will work out. You will see John and your family soon enough,* she told herself. Dorothy was learning to deal with life, but she was lonely, spent her time weeping, and lost interest in school. She studied only what she wanted and didn't care about the other subjects. Still she managed to do well and her knowledge of Greek and Latin helped her to win a scholarship to the University of Illinois.

Once in college, Dorothy changed in many ways. She observed the people around her who went to church. They did not seem concerned about the poor, while she still had a longing in her heart. Somehow she heard God's voice. But she didn't know where to find Him. She concluded she didn't need Him anymore. *But did God need her?* She wondered. *Where do I belong?* The churches she searched seemed to be doing little to fight injustice and help the struggling masses of humanity. God did not seem to be in the church people she met. She wanted no part of them. At school she scorned students who were pious, and religious people who seemed happy, yet seemed only to think of themselves. She hardened her heart and started to smoke, swear and take God's name in vain, in order to shock her friends, trying to push thoughts of religion away. She read the Bible but couldn't find anyone in her life who truly followed the words of Jesus. She wanted to help the poor and homeless. But she felt she was strong and didn't need any church to guide her and felt the religious church people she met were doing nothing to change things. She wanted to give herself to the cause of the poor and homeless in her own way but didn't know how to do so.

Chapter 9

God's Call

Only this I have found, that God made man right and he
hath entangled himself with an infinity of questions.
— *Ecclesiastes. 7:29*

After two years, her schooling ended when her father began to work for the *Morning Telegraph* in New York City. She had thought she didn't need her family, but realized she could not bear to be so far from them especially little John. So she left Chicago and moved to New York. As she gazed around her, she became aware that the poor of New York were suffering even more than those she had seen in Chicago.

Dorothy searched for a writing position, but jobs were scarce. To make it even worse, she hadn't finished college. After a long search, she finally was hired by a newspaper where she proposed writing a column and working for a very low salary to demonstrate how someone could live on five dollars week. She left her parents' home and found a room of her own.

Her little room was tiny and bleak. She had barely any space to move, but she learned that it was possible to live on a meager sum if one lived in the low-rent district and did not spend money on recreation, clothes, books or doctors. She wrote daily columns for the newspaper telling of her experiences and gradually was assigned other stories and given a better salary.

For a few years, this was Dorothy's life. Her heart ached for the poor. She went from one group to another trying socialism, anarchism, and communism. Nothing satisfied her longing. She joined group protests and marches, hoping to end human misery and even spent 10 days in jail after a march on hunger in Washington, where they went on a hunger strike. After six days of not eating, some were held down and forced to eat. Tubes were forced down their throats or noses. It was horrible, but all of these experiences helped her to better understand the plight of the poor.

Dorothy wanted to be free, not bound by rules. This led her to disobey many of God's laws. She felt she knew better how to fulfill her heart's longings. God's laws would have given her a purpose and direction for which she longed, but she did not understand this and assumed she knew better how to fulfill her heart's longings. So, mistaking unbridled freedom to be what her heart desired, she would say to herself *I am strong and the strong can make their own laws and live their own lives.*

Like the early lives of many saints, she fled from God. For a time, she could stifle her conscience. Then a time came when she could no longer endure the life she was leading. *There has to be something more to life,* she told herself. She struggled to find that way. She wanted to help people so she decided to try something new.

Chapter 10

Nursing

Your love for God is only as great as the love you have for
the person you love the least.
— *Dorothy Day*

It was 1918, she was twenty-one and the country was engaged in World War I. Since many nurses had left to join the armed forces, there was a need for them in the hospitals at home. Dorothy decided that nursing the sick was a way to care for others. She and her sister Della signed on as probationers at King's County Hospital in Brooklyn. Her first patient was a ninety-four-year-old woman who wouldn't allow the nurses to wash her. Whenever they entered the room or neared her bed carrying a pan of water and a cake of soap, she fought them and clawed at them as she screamed, "Go away. Leave me alone! Leave me alone!"

"Come now, let us help you," one of the other nurses said kindly, "Can't you see that we want to take care of you because we love you?"

Dorothy stood by the bed trembling with her hands reaching out to comfort, but she felt helpless.

"Love be damned," the little old lady cried, "I want my wig."

She pointed to the bald spot on her head where she only had a fringe of hair and she began to cry and rant again.

The nurse turned to Dorothy and said, "I don't know what to do. We let her have her teeth, but now she wants her wig. I don't see why they won't let her have it. I must talk to the head nurse. We can't go on like this."

Dorothy nodded her head as she followed along the corridor to the nurses' station. After much discussion, they convinced the head nurse that the woman needed more than soap and water and clean bed linen. She needed more than words of love. She needed to be respected as a person. She needed her wig! They searched the station and the room. They searched everywhere, but it seemed no one knew where it was.

The head nurse said, "We will give her this little lace cap. Maybe that will calm her down."

When they returned to the room and placed it on her head, the old lady stopped crying and smiled at them. Her fight was over, and Dorothy learned her first lesson. True compassion includes understanding, respect, and a special kind of love.

Dorothy had a hard time dealing with some other problems. Sometimes patients would spit at the nurses or be filthy in their ways. Dorothy would have to grit her teeth and hold her breath while caring for them. One afternoon, when she had been cleaning up filth all day, an angry patient threw her bedpan out on the floor spraying its contents all over Dorothy's uniform, shoes and stockings. She ran from the ward in tears and sat alone on a chair in the washroom, weeping uncontrollably. She knew she had done the unforgivable thing of running away from her duties, but she couldn't take it anymore. She no longer cared about the patients. She didn't care about anything. She didn't want to be a nurse. She ran to her room where she flopped across the bed and buried her face in the pillow, her tears soaking the pillow case as she sobbed.

The assistant superintendent heard about all this from another nurse. She went to the dormitory and knocked on the door. Dorothy jumped from her bed and opened it to let her in.

After putting an arm around her and wiping her tears, she said, "Dorothy, you have responsibilities as a nurse. You can make a change and help people. You must try to understand them. Sometimes it is very hard, but a nurse is doing God's work and you are a chosen person."

Dorothy stopped crying and listened and the words sank in. The next day she returned to her job and after a few days she gradually became used to the daily routine and troubles of being a nurse and learned to love the work. Dorothy had learned another lesson. A sense of duty means giving loving care without thinking of one's self.

While working at the hospital, Dorothy became friends with another young nurse, Miss Adams, who asked her to go to Mass in the chapel with her on Sunday. "Okay, I'll go with you," she said as she dragged herself out of bed to go to church. Dorothy found herself drawn to the faith that Mrs. Barrett had shown her so many years ago. The sun blazed through the stained glass windows as she knelt near the altar for the first time. After Mass was over, she looked to the statue of Jesus, pleading with Him to show her the meaning of life. Her earnest pleas drew her closer to the heart of God. Still, she waited for an answer to *Why am I here?*

Soon after she started working at the hospital, Dorothy met a charming young man who worked as an orderly. She fell in love with him. One day she told her sister, Della, who worked with her at the hospital, "Oh, Della, I love Lionel so much and I know he loves me, too. He has asked me to move in with him." In those days girls did not move in with their boyfriends unless they were married. Though Dorothy went to Catholic services with Miss Adams, she had a will of her own and did not care what the church or other people thought. She wanted to be with Lionel no matter what.

Meanwhile she came to realize that nursing, though she had come to love it, was not the answer for her. She was exhausted by the hours. She told her supervisor at the hospital that she was leaving. Because she, as well as her father and two brothers, wrote for newspapers, she felt that was her calling.

After she and her love, Lionel, lived together happily for a couple of months, Dorothy found out she was pregnant. She was happy but Lionel was not. He said he would leave her. "Dorothy, I told you before, I want no part of marriage or a baby. Go get an abortion or I will leave you."

"Oh, Lionel, please don't say that." she begged. She was torn apart. She didn't want to have an abortion, but she asked herself. *What can I do? I love Lionel more than anything. I need him. I can't give up my baby but I need Lionel.* Eventually, she gave in. A friend directed her to a woman in a little sordid back room apartment who removed her baby.

It didn't matter! She returned home to find Lionel gone forever. His note said, "I'm leaving town. There is no chance of a reconciliation between us."

"*What have I done?*" she cried. She knew she had made a mistake . . . and it was too late. It caused her heart to ache every minute of her life for the rest of her days. She would not speak of it to anyone then or ever again.

After a time, she met and married Berkeley Toby, a wealthy business man, who took her on a tour of Europe. This marriage lasted less than a year.

Chapter 11

Moving On

They that sow in tears shall reap in joy.
— *Psalms 126:5*

For the next few years, Dorothy did write and she also traveled to Europe on her own, ever conscious of the poor and destitute wherever she went. When she was twenty-two she came back to Chicago. There she shared an apartment with Blanche and Bea, two young Catholic girls she had recently met. Bea told her about "making a mission and praying for someone's intention." Dorothy thought, *What kind of foolishness is this?* They explained that a mission was a number of days devoted to extra prayer and that "praying for someone's intention" was a way of asking God to bless someone other than yourself.

The three girls used to sit on the couch in the living room at night discussing how to live their lives. Dorothy thought, *Bea and Blanche have faith in their God whom they worship, they have their saints to pray to, but I have nothing.* One night when she thought the others were asleep, she came home and walked into the darkened living room. There she saw Blanche kneeling down by a candle-lit table in the room saying her prayers. She stood still and stared at her friend, who was unaware of her, remembering

Kathryn's mother, Mrs. Barrett, praying in her bedroom many years before.

Touched by that moment, Dorothy began to read about the Catholic Church in the books the girls gave her. Her constantly growing love of the poor drew her to go more and more to Mass and benediction at the nearby cathedral where she finally saw people practicing love of neighbor. She became interested in the church but never joined it. Then a new friend, Mary Gordon, gave her a rosary. Dorothy put it in her purse, but she didn't know what to do with it. And it didn't mean anything to her.

After a few years spent writing and selling a novel she had written, Dorothy fell in love again. Her friends introduced her to Forster Batterham. Though they were not married, again this did not bother Dorothy who was still a free spirit. They moved in together to a little house on the beach. These were happy days and she didn't think much about going to church. But when she walked along the pathway to the village for the mail, she found herself praying again. Then she would reach into her jacket pocket and felt the little rosary Mary had given her, praying in her own words as she talked to God. She wanted to thank Him because she was so happy.

One sunny June day when the sky was blue and their hearts were light, Forster, Dorothy and two friends went on a picnic and then to the circus. That day, she knew for sure she was going to have a baby. She could hardly wait to be alone with Forster to tell him the news. It was so hard to keep the wonderful secret until they got home.

As they walked in the door, she hugged him and said, "Forster, we are going to have a baby!"

Forster stood still and stared at her. Tears filled Dorothy's eyes when he answered.

"Oh, Dorothy, you know I don't believe in bringing children into the kind of world in which we live. I don't feel I should be a father."

As the days passed, Forster did get used to the idea and in March, Tamar Teresa was born. He immediately loved this baby, who became a joyful little girl. In spite of what he had said, Forster was fascinated by his little daughter.

Dorothy would rock her little baby and hold her close as she had done many years before with her little brother John. When the weather got warm, they would take her to the sandy beach and dip her toes into the waves as they sang little songs to make her smile.

Though she was happy with her baby, Dorothy had some troubling thoughts. She remembered how she had never known about God or how to pray when she was little. She wanted her daughter to grow up loving God. She decided to have Tamar baptized in the Catholic Church. She discussed this with Forster, but he would not hear of it.

"No, Dorothy, I do not believe in God. I will not allow my daughter to be baptized," he declared whenever she mentioned it.

Dorothy knew in her heart what was best for her little girl. She felt that Baptism was the greatest gift she could give her. She worried herself sick about not being able to bring this blessing of God to her child. One day while out for a walk, she met a Catholic nun, Sister Aloysia. They became friends and Dorothy learned more about the Church. Finally, she decided she would go against Forster's wishes. In July, Tamar was baptized and Dorothy knew then that, she, too, should share the Catholic faith with her daughter. Adopting this faith, which she now believed in, meant there had to be changes in her lifestyle.

Living together without marriage was one of them. First, she and Forster would have to marry in the Church, but Forster also did not believe in the Church or in a marriage ceremony. He refused to consider it. Their life changed. Forster and Dorothy quarreled all the time. He did not understand this new Dorothy. *How can I choose between Forster and my new faith? I love Forster with all my soul.* Though it was almost more than she could bear, she knew she had to choose God. Forster left her.

Chapter 12

Lonely Days

The greatest challenge of the day is: how to bring about a
revolution of the heart, a revolution which has to start
with each one of us.
— Dorothy Day

Every day for over a year, as she cuddled her baby,
Dorothy would weep and pray. While her baby was
napping in her crib, she would kneel before a little table in
her living room and pray, with tears running down her
cheeks as she gazed at a little statue of Mary holding the
child Jesus.

"Dear God, please help me. I love Forster so much.
He is my life. How can I go on without him?" she pleaded.

For a long time there was a struggle in her heart, but
eventually, she knew it was over. Forster was gone for
good. He wasn't coming back but she never stopped loving
him.

She had chosen to follow Christ and now loved *Him*
with all her heart. She became a Catholic. Dorothy spent a
few years writing for various Catholic publications. Still,
she had no real direction in her life. She was still
powerfully overcome with concern for the poor she saw
around her, yet she didn't know how she should help.

It is hard to imagine what life was like at that time. A Depression had overtaken the world. Between 1929 and 1932, millions of Americans were out of work and had no place to turn, no way to pay their bills. Many were homeless, without enough to eat. Some people would walk the streets and knock on doors of nearby homes begging for food. Others waited in long soup lines. Dorothy was dismayed by all this. Seeking to help, she joined a hunger march of the jobless who stormed Washington where streets were closed to banish them. Finally, on December 8, 1932, the feast of the Immaculate Conception, the streets that had been blocked to them were opened. The marchers had delivered their message to the powers in Washington. They then returned to their homes with a glimmer of hope. *But what is the answer?* She wondered.

With tears in her eyes, as she headed for the train home, she moved slowly down the street. Somehow she found herself at the door of the beautiful church at the Shrine of the Immaculate Conception. She walked up the long aisle and knelt at the altar. Holding tightly to the rail, she stared at the golden crucifix.

As she wiped away the tears rushing down her cheeks, she pleaded, "Dear Jesus, show me how I can help. Open my eyes to see a way to use my talents for the poor. I've tried to figure this out for myself, but I need You. I don't know what to do."

As she knelt there she realized that after three years of being a Catholic she was still without direction. Though she had been going to Mass and Communion all along, she had no idea what it truly meant to live every day as a Catholic person.

Chapter 13

A New Direction

Where there is no love, put love and you will find love.
— *St. John of the Cross*

Dorothy took the train from the Washington station to her home in New York, looking forward to seeing her little Tamar. When she walked into the apartment, she was met by her brother and his wife, who shared the rooms. She also saw a short, stocky, man in a wrinkled suit, waiting for her. She collapsed on the sofa exhausted, hugging her little daughter.

The man reached out his hand to her and said, "I am Peter Maurin."

The tilt of his head and the warm glow in his eyes grabbed her attention.

"Come back tomorrow," she told him. "I am too tired to talk with you." Watching him go through the door, she wondered, *Who is this strange man? What does he want from me?*

Early the next morning as she was in the kitchen sipping her coffee, a knock came at the door. Peter walked in and as she listened to his words, she realized that she had found the answer that she had been seeking ever since she was eight-years-old. Knowing she had just come back from

Washington, Peter started talking non-stop about the problems of the federal government. He pointed out that the only way to solve the problems of the world was to study the teachings of Christ. Peter, a former monk, had a vision constructed on Gospel values. Through true Christian love, he felt individuals could rebuild the world. Dorothy thought, *Here is someone who feels like me.* Peter finally gave her the life purpose she was seeking. She knew why she was born.

Peter was dismayed by the limited Catholic education that Sister Aloysia had given her. "Dorothy, you must read the lives of the saints and books by Catholic scholars." he told her. "Catholics have a responsibility to help others and to take action against evil and injustice in the world."

WHAT DOROTHY SAID ABOUT INJUSTICE

"Those who cannot see the face of Christ in the poor are atheists indeed."

This was the call to action for which Dorothy had been waiting.

Peter eventually showed her how to see Christ in others, love the Christ in others, and have faith in Christ. Finally, she knew what God wanted her to do. She had found meaning for her life. And Dorothy, a journalist for leading Catholic journals, realized He wanted her to use her skills as a writer for His work. Peter, a journalist, himself, explained how they could do this.

Together they started a newspaper whose purpose was to call people's attention to the plight of the poor, the unemployed and the unemployable. The idea was, "Where there is no love, put love and you will find love." Dorothy had finally found the best way to use her talents. With only faith and hard work, with little money or office space, *The Catholic Worker,* which still exists today, was born in Dorothy's kitchen. Looking at the room around her, Dorothy lamented. "Peter, we have no money for all this."

"God sends you what you need when you need it. You will be able to pay the printer. Just read the lives of saints," Peter told her.

In May, 1933, 2,400 copies were sold and by 1936 it was 150,000. The newspaper was sold for one cent a copy to make it cheap enough so anyone could afford it and even free to anyone who did not have a penny. Peter and Dorothy wrote articles about labor, strikes, unemployment, factual accounts and essays. Dorothy protested against unfair pay and hiring practices, and worked to help others, in every way.

She gave her whole self over to the Lord. In the midst of the Great Depression, in May 1933, when the number of unemployed people was 13,000,000, she not only was the editor of *The Catholic Worker,* but she also started her first hospitality house. Gradually, many caring people joined her. At first they all lived together in a small apartment with the poor and homeless. The door was open from early morning till late at night. Each volunteer would take a turn cooking for everyone. Dorothy herself became not only a newspaper editor and newspaper vendor, but a cook and cleaner as well. There was ever-flowing coffee and "mulligan stew" for all who wandered in. Then another apartment was rented for ten women and later another for men. Eventually, a house was rented. As Peter had predicted, money was coming in steadily.

As the years passed, Dorothy's Houses of Hospitality could be found all over the United States and throughout the world. They accepted anyone needing aid for as long as they needed it with no limits on the time these homeless people were allowed to stay.

Dorothy was participating in strikes wherever she saw injustice.

She said, "We are able to 'endure wrongs patiently' for ourselves, but we are not going to be meek for others, enduring *their wrongs patiently.*" Dorothy was a fighter! She and her many followers went everywhere to perform the Works of Mercy, which included sheltering the homeless, clothing the naked, feeding the hungry, and visiting the imprisoned. They lived the lessons of love taught by Jesus but there is no preaching except by example. A crucifix on the wall of each home was the only evidence of the faith of those welcoming the guests.

To stand closely with those around her, she pledged herself to poverty. She felt you must live with the poor and share their sufferings. So Dorothy, along with her helpers, lived with the poor in apartments, hospices, and farms for the rest of her life.

Meanwhile, Tamar, who was the joy of her mother's life, was growing up. They lived together in Dorothy's various communities. She was a thoughtful little girl who asked things like, "Does the Blessed Mother mind if I say my prayers standing on my head?" and "How can I pray when I have to keep laughing?"

Tamar's life was different from the average little girl. Her mother was often away attending meetings with priests, scholars and workers. Through all this, Tamar learned sympathy and compassion for all suffering things. She lived in many homes because her mother's duties meant they often had to move. She attended various schools and was married when she was eighteen.

Chapter 14

Final Days

*Where are the saints to try to change the social order, not
just minister to slaves, but do away with slavery?*
— *Dorothy Day.*

For many years, Dorothy wrote for *The Catholic Worker*
and established "hospitality homes" and community
farms for the poor. She was strongly against war, feeling it
was not what Jesus taught and she vigorously protested
against it. She questioned, "Who would Jesus bomb? Are
not all men brothers?"

Though she earned money from her books and
articles over the years, and could have lived a more
prosperous life, she lived in poverty with the unloved,
sharing and teaching the love of God by her every action.
She has written 8 books and more than 320 articles for
journals and magazines as well as over 1000 articles for
The Catholic Worker newspaper.

Dorothy was full of compassion and fight. All that
she accomplished throughout her life is too much to tell
you here. It was a life totally connected with the life of
Jesus. She traveled throughout the world, sharing her love
of Jesus and the Catholic faith. She visited with Mother
Teresa and spoke with important officials as well as the

poor and suffering. Dorothy lived through three wars and the atomic age. She always concerned herself with suffering humanity in a world of turmoil. There are other books that will fill in the blanks for you. You may want to read them as you get older.

By March 1975, Dorothy was starting to slow down. She had problems with her heart and was often tired and weak. Peter had died many years before, so she put the paper into the hands of the young volunteers who had worked with them. She went to live in Maryhouse, one of her communities in New York City where she was loved and cared for. For the next few years she spent her days reading, listening to the radio, watching television and praying. The rosary, which she had long ago learned to say, was never out of her hands. It gave her comfort and often she remembered the day Mary had given her that first one and how, not knowing the prayers, she said it in her own way. She thought of how happy holding it had made her feel, as she carried it in her jacket pocket while living on the beach with Forster.

On the afternoon of November 29, 1980, Tamar came to visit her mother. It was a beautiful autumn day. The trees were still full of colorful leaves. As they sat together peering out at East Third Street filled with noise and teeming action, Dorothy slowly rocked in her chair and told her daughter how happy she was with her life.

Then, she turned her head and said, "Tamar, you know, I would love to have a cup of tea."

Tamar retreated into the kitchen where she heated the water and brewed a pot of the tastiest tea for her mother. Dorothy sipped the hot drink as they talked about her little grandchildren and Tamar's latest activities. She held her precious daughter's hand in hers and smiled.

At 5:30 P.M., suddenly without a warning, she closed her eyes and her heart just stopped beating. The moment was as quiet as sands through an hourglass. She now was with the Jesus she had loved for so long. Tamar wept as she gently clung to her mother.

Dorothy found the true meaning of life. Throughout the years she had found joy in being a true follower of Jesus. As the clouds of Heaven welcomed her, how joyful she must have been as Jesus held her close and smiled at his good and faithful servant.

On December 2, the Church of the Nativity was crowded as her grandchildren carried the casket. Tamar, Forster, and all her family as well as hundreds of friends, sadly prayed for her soul and thanked God for the gift of her life with them. She was buried at Resurrection Cemetery on Staten Island not far from where her fisherman cottage once stood.

Did little Dorothy's wish come true? Did she become a saint? In February 2000, she was declared *venerable* by the Catholic Church. Hopefully this will soon be followed by *beatification* and finally *sainthood*!

There were three things which qualified her. First, she lived what she believed. She combined charity with justice. She devoted her life to all the works of mercy. Second, she was committed to nonviolence. She believed in Jesus' words, "Love your enemies," challenging the conscience of the Church and its people. Third, she had courage, integrity, and was always faithful to the Gospel.

Dorothy once questioned, "Where are the saints who really care?" Many people today feel she was that saint herself. Some day we will know. Hopefully, when we do get to Heaven, we will find Dorothy, with Jesus at her side, welcoming us with a warm hug, as we thank her for showing us "how to get there."

Notes

The Catholic Worker Movement is grounded in a firm belief in the God-given dignity of every human person. It is committed to nonviolence, voluntary poverty, prayer, and hospitality for the homeless, exiled, hungry, and forsaken. It continues to protest injustice, war, racism, and violence in all forms every day.

There are over 185 Catholic Worker communities in thirty-seven U.S. states, six in three Canadian provinces. and fifteen in ten other countries. Each community is independent of the others in how they incorporate Catholic Worker philosophy and traditions. The newspapers of each community address current issues in light of Catholic social teaching.

Sayings

Your love for God is only as great as the love you have for the person you love the least.

— Mother Teresa.

They that sow in tears shall reap in joy.

— Psalm 126:5

Going, they went and wept, casting their seeds.

— Psalm 125:6-7

But coming, they shall come with joyfulness, carrying their sheaves.

— Psalm125:6-7

Only this I have found, that God made man right and he hath entangled himself with an infinity of questions.

— Ecclesiastes 7:29

The needy shall not always be forgotten, nor the hope of the poor perish forever.

— Psalm 9:18

O Lord, You are my God . . . for You have been a refuge to the poor, a refuge to the needy in their distress.

— Isaiah 25

As Christians, we are called to respond to the needs of all our brothers and sisters, but those with the greatest needs require the greatest response.
—U.S. Catholic Bishops' pastoral
letter on economic justice.

Where there is no love, put love and you will find love.
— St. John of the Cross

He who says he has done enough has already perished.
— St. Augustine

Perfect love casts out fear and overcomes hatred. All this sounds trite but experience is not trite.
— 1 John 4:17-19

We cannot love God unless we love each other, and to love we must know each other.
— Dorothy Day

We have all known the long loneliness and we have learned that the only solution is to love and that loves comes with community.
— Dorothy Day

Chronology

1897, November 8	Born in Brooklyn Heights, New York
1905	Family moved to California
1906, April 18	San Francisco earthquake
1906, April 25	Family moved back to New York
1911, May	Brother John was born
1913, September	Started at University of Illinois
1916	Joined parents in New York
1918, April	Entered nurses training King County Hospital1924 Met Forster Batterham
1926, March	Daughter Tamar was born
1932, December 8	Hunger Strike in Washington, D.C.
1932, December 9	Met Peter Maurin
1933, May	First issue of *Catholic Worker* newspaper

1933   First Hospitality House
                               opened

1949, June 15   Death of Peter Mauren

1977   Moved to Maryhouse, East
                               Third Street, NY

1980, November 29   Died

1980, December 2   Laid to rest at Resurrection
                               Cemetery, Staten Island.

The Corporal Works of Mercy

Feed the hungry

Give drink to the thirsty

Clothe the naked

Shelter the homeless

Comfort the imprisoned

Visit the sick

Bury the dead

The Spiritual Works of Mercy

Instruct the ignorant

Counsel the doubtful

Admonish the sinner

Bear wrongs patiently

Forgive injuries

Comfort the sorrowful

Pray for the living and the dead

The Eight Beatitudes of Jesus from

The Sermon on the Mount

Blessed are the poor in spirit

For theirs is the kingdom of heaven.

Blessed are they who mourn

For they shall be comforted.

Blessed are the meek

For they shall inherit the earth.

Blessed are they who hunger and thirst for righteousness

For they shall be satisfied.

Blessed are the merciful

For they shall obtain mercy.

Blessed are the pure of heart

For they shall see God.

Blessed are the peacemakers,

For they shall be called children of God.

Other Books of Inspiration by Claire Mohan

Mother Teresa's Someday

The Young Life of Mother Teresa of Calcutta

A Red Rose for Frania

The Way of the Cross, A Story of Padre Pio

Katie, The Young Life of Mother Katharine Drexel

The Young Life of Pope John Paul II

St. Maximilian Kolbe, The Story of the Two Crowns

The Story of Benedict XVI for Young People

Give Me Jesus

Joseph from Germany, The Life of Pope Benedict XVI for Children

The Young Life of Sister Faustina

Kaze's True Home, the Young Life of Mother Maria Kaupas

Made in the USA
Middletown, DE
20 March 2019